I KNOW YOU CAN ANNE!

Written and Illustrated by Che LaRhue

This book is dedicated to:

Betty, my Super Fantabulous grandma and to my

Kimora Dragon and Zyla Bear. It's because of you guys I know I can

Brooklyn Publishing Group

Visit our Website @ www.BrooklynPublishingGroup.com

For information or for bulk purchases, please email brooklynpublishers@gmail.com

Made in the U.S.A.

10 9 8 7 6 5 4 3 2 1

ISBN 978-0-9824460-2-7

Anne a **Bright** and **Curious** Girl

Wanted to know what she could be in this

BIG BIG World

Anne *Giggled* and *Laughed*

Before she asked...

Do you think I
can be a
Teacher?

You're **smart** and *know your*

ABC's and 123's

You'll be the best teacher you *can* be.

You want to be a teacher?

I know you can!

Do you think I
can be a
Fireman?

You're **courageous** and **fearless**

When *you hear* the fire alarm ring

When you put your mind to it

You *can do* anything

You want to be a fireman?

I know you can!

Do you think I
can be a
Musician?

You **sing** beautifully and

know the **beat**

You *definitely* put me on my feet

You want to be a Musician?

I know you can!

Do you think I can be a Nurse?

You're **caring**  and **helpful**

I know you'll be the *best* Nurse you can be

You want to be a nurse?

I know you can!

Do you think I
can be an
Actress?

You're **beautiful** and

talented

You'll have a *million* fans

You want to be an actress?

I know you can!

Do you think I
can be a
Doctor?

You're

intelligent

and

trustworthy

Whether the cold or the flu *you'll know* what to do
You want to be a doctor?

I know you can!

Do you think I
can be an
Inventor?

You're **clever** and have **good** ideas

And **great** plans

You want to be an Inventor?

I know you can!

Do you think I
can be a
Writer?

You're **creative** and *have a* vivid

imagination

You want to be a writer?

I know you can!

Do you think I
can be a
Policeman?

You're **honest** and know right from wrong

I know you'll get *the job* done

You want to be a policeman?

I know you can!

Now that Anne knows that she can
She knows you can too
You can be anything or do anything
You want to do

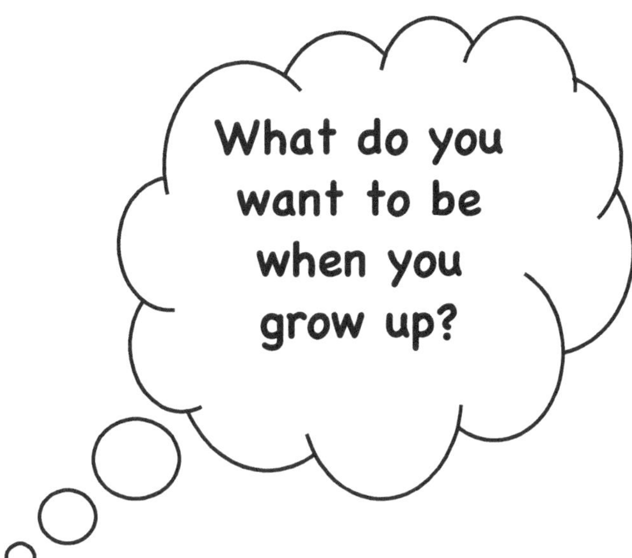

My name is ____________________

I am ____________________ and ____________________

I want to be a ____________________________

Anne Knows You Can!

www.ingramcontent.com/pod-product-compliance
Lightning Source LLC
LaVergne TN
LVHW070226110826
845147LV00003B/653
9780982446027

I Know You Can, Anne! This book reminds the kid in all of us that we can be anything! From a clever Inventor to a jazzy Musician the many faces of Anne serve as inspiration. With inspiring and enlightening words, this picture book has great gift appeal for new baby, graduation, celebrating milestones, or just letting that special little girl know that they can like Anne.

Look for more books about Anne:

Anne Can! ABC

Anne Can! 123

Anne Can! Sing

Anne Can! Dance

BROOKLYN PUBLISHING GROUP

THE BROOKLYN PUBLISHING GROUP

Made in the U.S.A. 10 9 8 7 6 5

ISBN 978-0-9824460-2-7

For information or for bulk purchases, please email brooklynpublishers@gmail.com

Visit our Website @ www.BrooklynPublishingGroup.com

Lockdown Baby

Laura Feldman

Svetlana Belova